I'm Curious About
Michael Phelps

Daisy White

THE I'M CURIOUS ABOUT PICTURE BOOK SERIES TEACHES YOUNG READERS ABOUT THE WORLD'S COOLEST HISTORICAL FIGURES, DISCOVERIES, AND EVENTS.

CHECK OUT THE ENTIRE COLLECTION, PERFECT FOR THE CURIOUS READER:

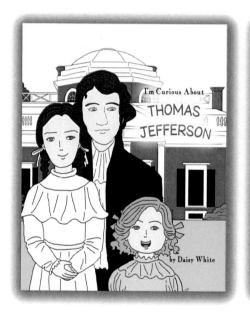

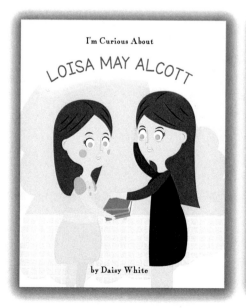

His lungs screaming, Michael Phelps clung to the edge of the pool gulping for air. He had just failed to swim underwater. Again. With hot tears in his eyes, he screamed to his older sister in frustration, "I can't do it Whitney! I'm 7 years old, and I can't even swim underwater. I'll never be a great swimmer like you!"

As his older sister eases his doubts, Michael's swimming instructors spoke amongst themselves, deciding how to proceed with the young swimmer's lessons. "Let's go ahead and call it a day, Michael. We will pick up where we left off tomorrow," one of the instructors tells him.

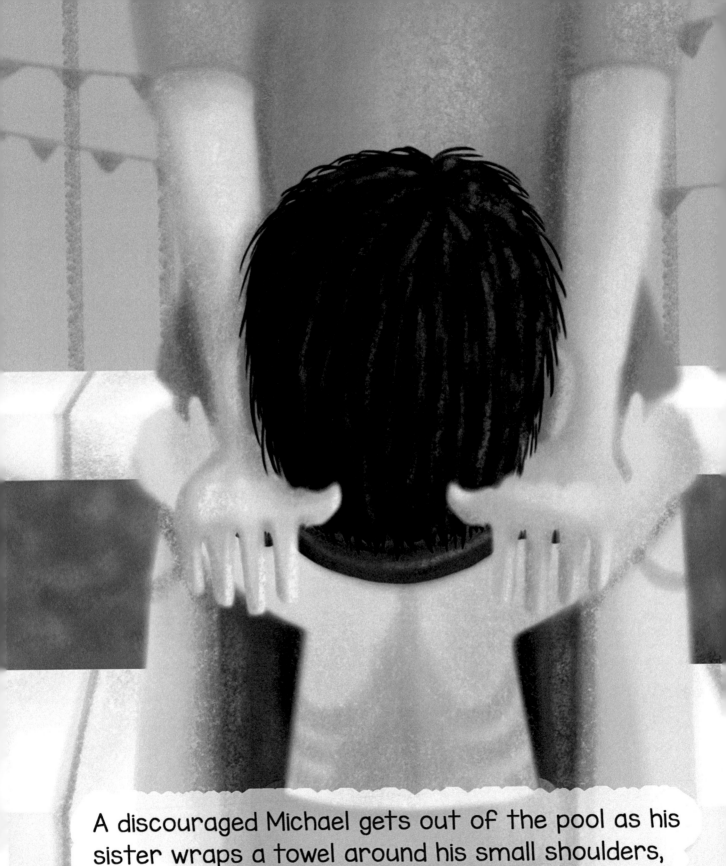

A discouraged Michael gets out of the pool as his sister wraps a towel around his small shoulders, and they head home.

That night, Michael goes quietly to his bedroom and closes the door behind him. As he lays in his bed, he looks around his room at all the remarkable swimmers that fill his walls. It's his dream to be a great swimmer, possibly even the best. But how could he when taking that plunge underwater makes him choke up and panic?

A light knock as his door shifts his thoughts. "Come in" Michael says. Whitney comes in and sits beside him on his bed. They are silent for a moment.

"Michael, did you know that when I was 9, I was afraid to jump off the diving boards the first couple of times I climbed up there? It was like the water was doubting me. I kept holding myself back before I even jumped in the water. I was afraid. Not just of the taunting water beneath me, but also the constant fear of failure in front of me.

It's okay to be scared, Michael. It's okay to be discouraged. It's even okay to lose. But it's not okay to give up. Don't give up on your dreams because of your fear of failing or not being good enough. You have greatness inside you. Go out and show it."

With that, Whitney walked out of his room and closed the door behind her.

Michael Phelps took a few deep breaths trying to calm his nerves. As he got up on the stand, he stretched and jumped. Swinging his arms rapidly and ignoring the ringing in his ears, Michael suctioned his goggles and adjusted his swim cap.

Eight short years later, and overcoming all the fears of the water he had once had, these words swim in his thoughts as he prepares for the biggest race of his life. Qualifying in this race would secure his spot on the United States Olympic Team.

With the shot of the start gun, he leaped outward. His arms breaking the surface as if an arrow being shot from a bow.

Catapulting himself, he focused all his energy on this swim. With all his strength, he pulled back the water, willing himself to go faster. His only thought was to push harder. As he took breaths above the surface, he caught glimpses of his opponents. They were close, and thoughts of losing this race quickly rushed into his head.

Heart beating wildly and muscles aching from the intense strain, Michael forced his body to increase their pace. He knew it would be close as he stretched his fingers out and touched the wall to finish the race.

PHELPS MICHAEL
UNITED STATES   51.21

LE CLOS CHAD
SOUTH AFRICA   51.44
OROTYSHKIN EVGENY
USSIA   51.44

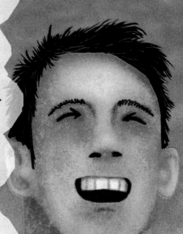

Coming up for a relieving breath, he immediately looked at the board to see his name on top. He had not only won the race; he had solidified his spot on the American Olympic team! He was becoming the youngest male Olympian the United States had had in 68 years time. Michael couldn't have been more excited and more nervous in his life. His journey was just beginning.

Michael went to his first Olympics in 2000. Although he didn't medal in any of his events, the experience made him even more dedicated and motivated to compete on the Olympic team again. With more time and vigorous training, Michael became a stronger swimmer.

He happily made it to the 2004 and 2008 Olympics. By the end of his third Olympic games, Michael became the first person to ever win a total of eight Olympic gold medals in a single Olympic Games. Michael's hard work was paying off. He quickly became known as the best swimmer in the world.

"I want to do it one more time, coach!" Breathless and tired, Michael begged for one more swim.

His coach took a hard look at him. Having already been training for six hours, he contemplated on whether or not to call it a night. Today hadn't been a good day for Michael. His swim times had just been…off. His coach thought a moment, "Oh, alright, Michael. But only one more swim. Then we need to give it a rest for the day."

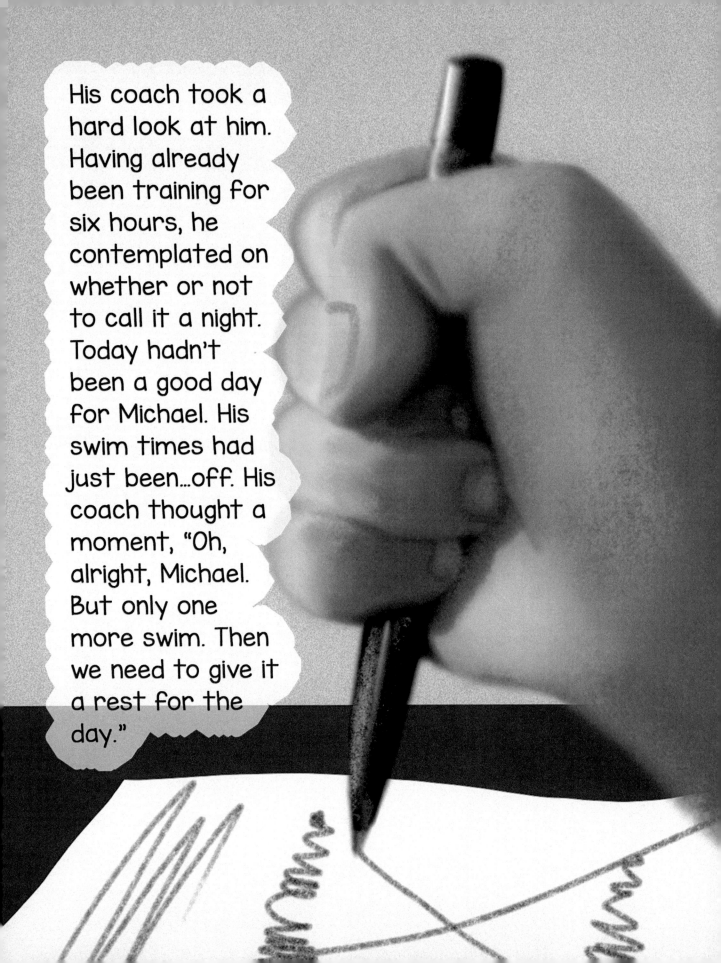

Michael plunged in the pool. His muscles screamed from the long hours of training that day, but he didn't care. He pushed through the pain willing himself to go faster. Giving this swim every bit of energy he had left, he touched the wall signaling the finish to the day's training.

Breathless and tired, he listened attentively as his coach told him his time.

"Yes! Yes, yes, yes!" Michael screamed with a sudden burst of energy and splashing in the water to celebrate his time.

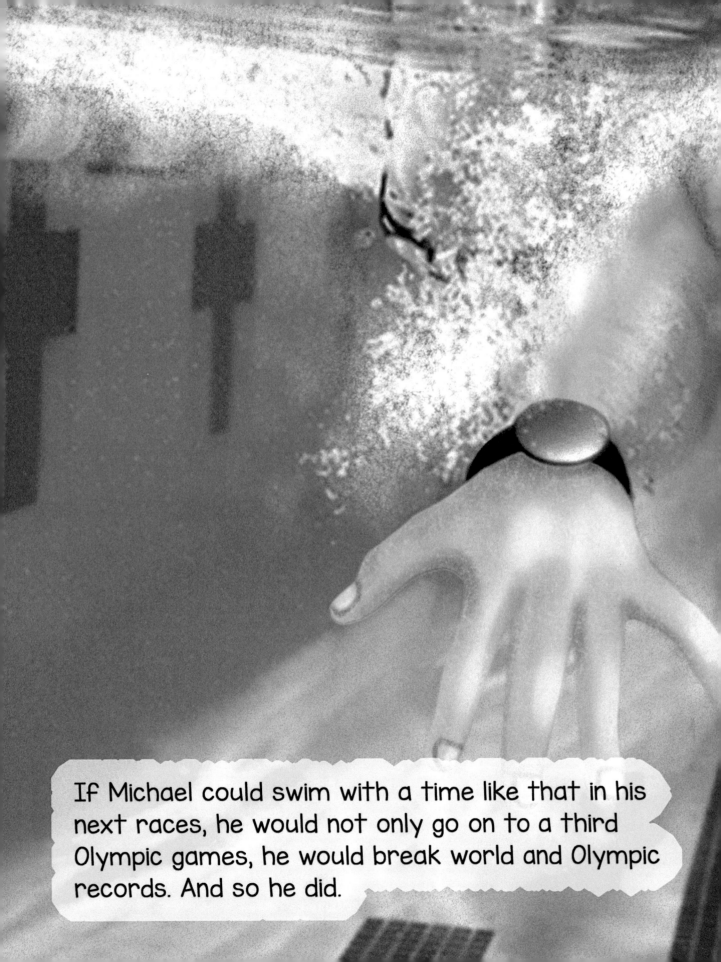

If Michael could swim with a time like that in his next races, he would not only go on to a third Olympic games, he would break world and Olympic records. And so he did.

Michael Phelps went on to participate in not just a third but a fourth Olympic game as well. When all was finished, he had won 23 gold medals and 28 medals total spread over four Olympic games.

At the end of his fourth Olympics, he retired the most successful Olympic medal earner in recorded history. *Not too bad for a kid who couldn't swim underwater at seven,* Michael thought with a broad smile.

Made in the USA
San Bernardino, CA
07 May 2019